# Our Voices:

A Collection of Wisdom from
Aquinas College TRiO Students

●

Edited by Brian Parsons
with Ann Karasinski & Julie Bevins

Cover design by Devon Klomp

# Chapbook Press

Chapbook Press
Schuler Books
2660 28th Street SE
Grand Rapids, MI 49512
(616) 942-7330
www.schulerbooks.com

Printed at Schuler Books in Grand Rapids, MI on the Espresso Book Machine®

ISBN 13: 9781936243532
ISBN 10: 1936243539

Our Voices
© Aquinas College 2013

| | | |
|---|---|---|
| Student Support Services | Madeleine Burns | Christian Baker |
| Brian Parsons | Marin Haffey | Leah Nawrocki |
| Ann Karasinski | Catherine Biewer | Jessica McCormick |
| Julie Bevins | Tyler Nadeau | Thomas Serna |
| Jill Straub | Ashley Browe | Chelsea Maslar |
| Abby Samotis | Danielle Ames | Sarah Robinson |
| Ashley Mikolajczak | Yasmeen Ahmed | Cecilia Kellogg |
| Robert Bennett | Katelyn Padalino | Mayra Monroy |
| Mercedes Settlemyre | Emily McAfee | Shelby Wittum |

*To the TRIO students at Aquinas College,*
*who bring their true selves every day.*

# Contents:

# *Introduction*

This project really began just over a year ago at a dinner amongst friends and colleagues as we pondered what could we as a staff do to help our students in the Student Support Services program. At some point in the conversation, Ann Karasinski leaned over to me and said, "Have you ever thought about doing a book with your students?" Her question seized me, because I had been doing that, and only that. Just thinking and not actually doing; making the same excuses internally students make all the time for why a project just wasn't happening. So over the next few months I began to think of what was the purpose of this endeavor?

Community.

Too often I would meet with the 40 or so program students assigned to me and marvel at the strength and resolve of the young person sitting across from me and I would form these bonds with them. But those bonds did not extend beyond my walls typically to getting to know other students in our program assigned to different specialists unless they were involved in other projects with us. Over time I began to wonder what their stories were. I had this desire to listen, to be present, and learn from our students. And thus, this book began.

The individuals who have so graciously shared their stories in this book are indeed brave souls for agreeing to follow my dream with this project despite not knowing fully what they were getting themselves into. They did so with no tangible rewards promised and no reprieve from the other responsibilities that tugged at their time and energy. So I owe them some gratitude for trusting in me. I hope this book can be a point of pride for these young authors and as a guide for their fellow TRiO students, both currently with us, and those who are still to come.

We asked the students to answer the following prompt, "What it feels like to ..." and then we got out of the way and let them create. A lot of them wrote about issues that affect them as students at Aquinas and others referenced their early childhood experiences and how that has shaped who they are today. I believe the words and emotions contained herein represent what any student on this campus could be potentially feeling. So perhaps these stories can be used as a starting point for future conversations between students and realize we are not alone in our feelings.

And if their stories can help further bring us together as a community then this whole project, which began at the urging of a friend, will all be worth it.

~ Brian Parsons

# *Playing in the Dirt*

## Abby Samotis

Many people may not have the opportunity to know what it's like to grow up with dirt under their nails. However, this has been the case in my life. Just recently I realized what impact dirt has had on my life and the role it plays in the person I am today. Although dirt is not technically an adjective it has acted as one throughout my life and has most definitely described, modified, and defined me.

The first syntactic role of an adjective is to describe a noun. Dirt has described me since I was a little girl where I'd most likely be found running through the rows of my family's garden, looking for butterflies and tip-toeing under sunflowers. It was common that my toddler pigtails were accompanied by dirty knees and a farmer's tan only a diaper would leave behind. Till this day, even though my tan lines have changed a bit, and now I topple over most sunflowers, my summers are still accompanied by dirty knees and fingernails. Dirt has become a substance that not only finds its way onto my skin, but into my character.

The second syntactic role of an adjective is to modify a noun. My relationship with dirt escorted me into my teenage years where I worked at a local flower shop. The countless hours spent weeding, pruning, and watering were hours that taught me the importance of hard work, developed my creativity, and strengthened my love for nature. My experiences with delighted customers including tearful brides, freckled faced children, and a few persistent elders filled my summers with life changing memories. Throughout these memories a singular characteristic always stood out, dirt. The dirt in my garden has seen all sides of me. My emotions have contributed salty tears watering the roots of my coneflower, echoing laughter on the swaying butterfly bush, and stomps of stubbornness on the invasive weeds. However, my garden never lets me leave with a negative attitude. Kneeling in the dirt, weeding and pruning, is the most therapeutic aspect of my life. It has modified my outlook on life knowing great things come from hard work, and that even a little sprout of green can turn into a remarkable flower.

The third syntactic role of an adjective is to define. Little did I know when I was making friends with the butterflies as a pig-tailed girl, my dirty little knees would define where my life went. After high school, I started a Sustainable Business degree at Aquinas College. The degree was a perfect combination of two of my favorite things, community and the environment. It is adequately preparing me for my future dream of owning my own sustainable greenhouse. The flower shop will be lined with local art, feature local musicians throughout the year, and hold workshops for community members to educate them on native plant species and horticultural practices. The greenhouse will partner with local classrooms, empowering children to get in touch with nature and breathe fresh air! I hope that my business will teach community members the importance of Mother Nature, and inspire people to get a little dirt under their nails.

In nature's eyes dirt is a precious substance and Mother Nature takes her time crafting dirt. It actually takes more than 500 years to create 1 inch of topsoil. Can you imagine working that long on something to create so little? Dirt is defined as a substance that soils someone or something, and to say the least he nailed it. Dirt has described, modified, and defined me and I am more than happy it spoiled me with its lessons along the way, or should I say soiled.

# Away From the Farm

## Ashley Mikolajczak

Anyone who knows me knows I am not equipped to live in the city. I was born and raised in the more country part of my small home town. I grew up fishing, off-roading, and playing in the mud. And then I went out to my aunt's farm, where I've spent every summer playing with puppies, maintaining bunnies, walking llamas, socializing hogs, chasing kitties, and riding and training horses. From sun up until well after sun down I'm out working with the critters. Whether mucking out stalls, feeding the many hungry mouths, or having fun hitting the trails bareback. I only ever really go indoors to eat, shower, sleep, or let the little dogs out back when I'm the only one there. Other than that it's go-go-go outside getting stuff done all day long. I love walking "my" pig around the yard, riding my horse bareback all over the place, keeping the other horses in practice with riding, training young/unbroken horses or introducing the older ones to something new, and watching the llamas be so excited to be taken out of their area into the front yard.

I've grown used to having these critters in my life, depending on me for a clean area, food, water, and attention. I wake up sometimes before dawn and am outside with my four-legged best friends, and I don't come inside until usually long after dark. Then it's a shower, midnight cookies if her boys are there, and go to bed for a few hours before starting another day.

Then I came to Aquinas, and everything was so different. I have no critters to be with here, no bunny cages to clean or stalls to muck. No hay to throw to the critters and no pigs to even just watch. It's all classes, homework, and study. And when that's done I hardly know what to do as I'm usually stuck in my dorm since I didn't bring a car here. The gym will only occupy me for about 20 minutes before I can't stand it anymore. That left me with one other option to help cure my boredom, and I hardly ever turned to this in high school. I started hanging out with the few friends I've made here, having met from living in the same building or having been introduced. That's helped me better adjust to not living in the country, and it helps cure my boredom every now and then. I've also started using the internet much more than I used to. I'm still not fully adjusted to city-living, and I eagerly look forward to a summer with my animal buddies and dirt roads.

The friends I've made aren't many at all, but we get along just fine because we have the same interests, likes and dislikes, or we're here for the same major and in the same classes. I'm not a people person at all and I'm usually shy with some bolder moments, but I get along with those I can relate to. Having met and befriended them, I felt like I was 'broadening my horizon' as a high school teacher of mine always liked to say. I was never lonely at home with my animals, even if I was the only human there. I came here and had no critters, so until I'd met these friends I did at times feel a little lonely, but that was normal for me as I usually did at my parents' house without all the wonderful creatures with me to keep me company and occupied.

I found some different things I have started to frequent on campus. One being going to the Moose to work on homework and my favorite, get my special coffee. I always get a single, with a double shot espresso, chocolate, chia, and toasted marshmallow flavoring. It's helped me motivate myself to finish homework, readings for class, and write or edit papers. Another place I'll visit is the Corner Café for a different setting and different food as I don't particularly care for the cafeteria. Usually I go alone because I know that'll be better for me to get stuff done, and I don't mind being on my own.

I've always been a more solitary being, but I needed these few friends to keep me sane and help push me through my first year. They aren't the same as my furry friends, but they are here for me in the city when my farm family isn't. They've helped me get through my first year with the shock of lifestyle change, and I know I'll remain friends with them throughout my time at Aquinas if not after as well.

# Like a Fish Out of Water

## Robert Bennett

Life for me was never really easy growing up; there was always one obstacle or another. So it wasn't a big shocker that when I came to Aquinas I found another one waiting for me. The only difference between the past obstacles and the one I faced here was that it affected me more on an emotional level.

I was born in Detroit, Michigan, a place that has a perpetual bad reputation from its depictions in the media. But for me it wasn't that bad. I spent most of my life there and sure it had its rough edges and crime streak but what city doesn't. To me it was home and I had grown accustomed to it. It was also a place where African Americans are the majority, so it was strange when I came to Aquinas College and found out I was actually the minority. The population of African Americans on campus could be counted and named off by the handful. The color difference was the beginning of the culture shock I had begun to experience. There was also a shift in culture; people talked and acted differently, it was like stepping into another world. People were always smiling and saying Hi to me when I walked past them; I thought it was so weird at first. It took many weeks for me to get comfortable with the different personalities.

But still I felt weird being here, I couldn't quite fit in with the people around me. It always felt we were on two different pages, speaking two different languages. In fact, it was exactly like that when I engaged in conversations with people because I always got confused by some of the references they were using, especially when it came to media. We didn't listen to the same music, or grow up the same way, it was totally strange. It took me a while to get all the 80's movie references or what Nutella was. Back home the movies and TV shows I grew up watching were all black centric like *Friday, Moesha, Sister Sister, That's so Raven* and many more. And no one really got the jokes that my friends from back home would laugh at. Luckily when it came to cartoons there was a level we could all relate on.

I felt like I was in a different country and I was only two hours away from home. At Aquinas I felt lonely and like I really wasn't able to connect with anyone. I joined the black student union on campus hoping to find people who could relate. This didn't work out how I planned because they all seemed to make smooth transitions; some were even from the Grand Rapids area. I tried to be friends with them outside of meetings and events but there were only like 6 people and most of them were older and lived off campus. So communication was lacking there as well. This was a paradox to me because I am very cool with everyone, have an inviting and fun personality and am good at making friends but inside of me something was off. But all these racial things were just the tip of the iceberg for me feeling ostracized at a college that was known for its sense of community.

When I came to Aquinas I already knew what I wanted to major in and there was nothing that would change my mind. Theatre was my passion. The funny thing about the major I had chosen was that I never had any experience with it coming in. So when I started classes I felt inferior to all the other students who were involved with Theatre since high school or before that. I was literally a blank slate but I was eager to learn. In all my life I have never really been the quiet kid in class, who just sits and takes notes. How quickly that changed when I began to take acting classes. This became another strange world for me. And another language that separated me from everyone else. I couldn't relate to the kids in the theatre department about theatre nor could I talk to the kids outside the department about it. I was stuck in-between and I was beginning to have doubts about the school, about my major. As the school year went on, I kept fighting my inner thoughts and soon I overcame those feelings when I started to get more involved with the school. I became more involved with the black student union by taking a more active role and kept in contact with the members outside of class. I took the initiative to befriend more people even though we spoke two different languages, but the more we talked the more we found things in common and learned more things. I auditioned for my first play and though I was nervous from head to toe, and pretty sure that I would fail I still got a part in the show. Life began to settle down, it began to get easier. I was starting to smile more, and have more fun.

I found my place at Aquinas and I am really happy to have chosen this school.

# Being a First-Generation AQ Student

## Mercedes Settlemyre

Never in a million years did I think I'd be going to college, let alone one like Aquinas. I didn't know what college was really like besides what I saw on television shows and movies. In most movies they never really show what it's like in a classroom, just what happens outside of it. Take the movie "Pitch Perfect" for instance. You're never really watching the actors sitting in classrooms, but instead you watch them go to singing competitions and party. My mother and father never went to college and I didn't have any older siblings to show me how college would be. To be completely honest, I was scared. I'm a first-generation college student with a divorced family. My parents divorced when I was eight years old, when I didn't really understand anything. At that age I wasn't thinking about college, I was just curious about who I was going to play outside with or what lunch was going to be.

All through grade school, up until my junior year of high school, I didn't really ever think about what college I was going to go to or what I wanted to study. At my high school we took a prep class for the ACT, and then had days where only the juniors would come in to get tested. Once my senior year rolled around, everything was kicked into high gear. My high school gave us pamphlets on how to apply for FAFSA. When I went to file for financial aid, I pretty much did it myself; my mom gave me her information and said here you go. Luckily, I already knew how to do it by following what my high school gave me. My bowling coach here at Aquinas helped me get my application in on time, which was wonderful. My parents never really knew how to help me, so they just let me do everything and just worried about how much everything would cost once I was done.

Being a first-generation college student I've already experienced many struggles. For example, I don't have a family member to really understand what I have to do and what college is like. I've had struggles finding ways to pay for college. My mother's boyfriend recently left her last summer before my first year of college and she didn't have a steady job, so I had to work really hard to find scholarships and get a full time job in the summer.

Academically, having to deal with the workload has been quite the struggle also. In high school the way that I went about doing homework didn't quite work when I first got to Aquinas and I had to change how I studied and how I managed my time. Being a part of SSS has definitely helped me find ways that work for me. The best thing about all of this is that I have a great set of family and friends supporting me even if they don't understand what I have to do to become a successful college student. I've made a few good friends since I've been here at AQ, and whenever I'm struggling with being away from home or need some help studying for a test, they're always the first ones there with open arms. I don't think I'd be able to make it through this first year without them.

I hope that with me going to college and being able to show that certain things are possible, I hope my sister one day will follow in my footsteps and do what most people think is impossible. Since coming to college and being involved with the bowling team and having some great professors, I've learned that having people to lean on and actually asking for help when I'm struggling with something isn't such a bad thing. Not only can I manage my time a little better than how I did in high school, but I can also ask for help when needed.

# Being Alone

## Madeleine Burns

When people think of the word "alone" they usually think of it as a bad thing, a thing to be scared of. I was one of these people when it came to college. Someone scared that they weren't going to make any friends. Someone afraid that college just wasn't going to work out.

Throughout my life I experienced moments where I thought I was all by myself, like being afraid of the dark when I was little or being nervous to ride the school bus for the first time. In reality though, I always had my mom and siblings to depend on. Coming to Aquinas however, I was leaving the core people I had always had by my side. At Aquinas, I didn't know a single person. It was a world I had never experienced, something that I only dreamed of but never truly realized until Orientation. It was then that I finally recognized what it felt like to be alone.

I had been anticipating it, the moment when my family would leave to go back home and when I would join the rest of the incoming first years in the rest of the day's activities. The goodbyes were a few minutes, but it only felt like seconds before I watched them leave out the door. I stood there in the gymnasium wondering what to do next. Part of me wanted to run out and say one more goodbye, to prolong this moment from happening. But that wouldn't change the reality of it. I was alone in a crowd of strangers.

I knew my roommate just from the morning activities, so I went to find her. As I searched, the recognition of being on my own was exciting but at the same time absolutely terrifying. Being the oldest of my siblings, I really didn't know what to expect from college. Sure I had seen movies and toured a few other campuses, but actually being here was completely foreign. I tried not to let it get to me, but while I searched for my roommate, I fought back the tears that would escape me if I were to dwell on the thoughts of just how scared I was.

As the weekend progressed, the reality of being at college began to sink in. I started to pick up on the layout of campus, and with all of Orientation activities, I really hadn't had time to worry about anything but what I was doing at the moment. I realized that everyone else around me was in the same boat. We had all left our families, friends, and loved ones to come to college. We all had a fresh start.

The moment when it finally all came together for me was Pond Reflection at the end of Orientation. When the people in my group all admitted what they were afraid of and how they were feeling just as alone as I was, but in different ways. One person expressed their stress about their financial situation while another group member told everyone how sad they were to be apart from their significant other. The last person was from all the way across the country and had a sick parent at home. They knew that coming to Aquinas was the best thing for them, but they felt like they were abandoning everyone they loved. We all expressed our feelings as if we had known each other for years instead of three days. We didn't say anything after someone spoke, but the silence was understanding enough.

To me, this was comforting in an unexpected way. It allowed me to see that I wasn't really alone now, because together we all had each other. The next few weeks I kept this in the back of my mind, and before I knew it, I became really good friends with most of the people in my group.

Being alone isn't always a bad thing. It's a breath of fresh air to be by yourself and discover who you are. I have learned so much about what I can accomplish and what I believe in, and have made amazing friends that I wouldn't trade for anything. Coming to Aquinas is one of the best decisions of my life, one in which I didn't allow my fear to stop me despite how scary it was to be alone. Because you're never alone for very long.

# Finding a Home on Campus

## Marin Haffey

I'm a junior studying elementary and early childhood education at Aquinas. I am part of the Trio Student Support Services (SSS) program and could not be happier with the decision I made to join. Not only have I received different services within the past three years but I have also formed many wonderful friendships in the process. This is my story.

My freshman year I came in to SSS knowing that I had accommodations from my high school that carried over to college and that I could utilize the services. I had a great relationship with the resource teachers in my high school and hoped that college would be similar. But I had to wait. The first few weeks of freshman year were confusing. I felt lost, like I could not escape my antisocial roommate. She always stayed in the room but did not like to talk to me. I made other friends in my hall but I needed somewhere else to go where I felt safe and supported. Finally I was accepted into the SSS program and wanted to know more about it.

I entered Wege 110 and was greeted by the fabulous June Stevenson at her big fancy desk. I introduced myself and she explained some of the services that they offer. I knew this would be a great place for me. Towards the middle of the semester I found myself visiting SSS often just because I liked to talk to people. June would usually stop and listen to me ramble about my day, celebrate in my successes and comfort me in times of stress. Brian Parsons, one of the advisors, would joke around with me and always made my day. I liked SSS not just for the resources but also the community and knowing that someone who cared about me would always be there.

My sophomore year SSS started a peer mentoring program. I was offered a position as a freshman mentor and was excited. I wanted freshmen to have an experience with SSS like I did, not to be afraid of it or feel like you are taking advantage of your resources but mostly, to always have someone to talk to. In this case that someone was me, a student who had been in their position the year before. I was very excited to help new students get acclimated to Aquinas and act as a mentor and friend.

A lot of my mentees were a little less enthusiastic and thought that the meetings were a waste of time. Some of the freshmen stuck with me by coming to our meetings, engaging in conversation, and not just using me for the free coffee. Since we got to know each other on a personal level, I have remained good friends with all of these students. As a mentor I built up a foundation of trust and friendship with these students.. I consider these mentees good friends. I still enjoy meals together and checking with them on a regular basis. They were the head of my cheering squad and never missed a show when I played my ukulele at open mic nights at the Moose. One time we even met up over the summer for a trip to the zoo.

The other part to my job at SSS was working in the office. I got to know the students who came in on a regular basis like my best friend Jessie McCormick who shared my love for bothering June. When I started the mentor program I was not expecting to form such strong friendships but now I can't imagine it any other way.

Many staff members have been with me through it all like June, Brian, La Tonia Plunkett, and Gary K. During my junior year I met Julie Bevins who always makes my day, and Jill Straub who is not just a wonderful person but is also the owner of my favorite on campus dog, Archer. I have grown to love the staff here and every day I am blessed that I have these people in my life. The magnificent friendships and bonds I have formed have been a huge impact on my time at Aquinas and I would not be where I am today without Student Support Services.

# Being Homeschooled

## Catherine Biewer

Homeschoolers are an estimated 3% of the population. I am one of them. People are often surprised when they are told I was homeschooled. Like most minorities, we come with a plenitude of stereotypes. Sometimes we're marked as naturally being well-rounded, intelligent people, who think they're smarter than the rest of the population. Other times we're marked as being uneducated bigots. The stereotype most promulgated though is that we're somehow more unsocial than the rest of society. Although sometimes the stereotypes are true for select cases, it is often interesting for me to deal with all the questions and misunderstandings when I don't fall in one category or the other. When I came to Aquinas College, I wasn't sure how I would be treated. College has been a little of an adjustment, but so far my homeschool experience has benefited me here.

People are often curious what being homeschooled was like for me. Growing up, I lived in the country on eight acres of land with my parents and five younger siblings. We never found it strange that we stayed home to do school or that we didn't get to see our friends every day. It was normal and we were content. In the mornings, my mother would wake us up. She would make breakfast for the youngest children, but the older children were expected to make it themselves. At a young age, I became quite the expert in toasting bread, frying fresh eggs, and cooking up pancakes and waffles. It never occurred to me that other kids wouldn't normally do that every morning. After breakfast, we would do our school according to how old we were. When we were young, my mom would sit down with each child and go over subjects such as phonics, English grammar, and Latin & Greek words. She would read historical fiction books to us, as well as the occasional Dr. Seuss. When I was older, my mother gave me the books I needed and an optional schedule. It was essentially up to me to teach myself. Some mornings I would have an online Latin class. I would then do algebra problems, then switch to reading classic literature for a couple hours, then perhaps practice piano for a while. It varied by day.

This schedule may seem foreign to the other ninety-seven percent of the population. However, for me, having a strict school schedule was foreign. I was never tested. I never had to write reports or essays. I was allowed to write whatever I wanted, whenever I felt like writing, such as blogs and creative fiction. It was all very relaxed learning; I never really felt pressed to quickly memorize and regurgitate facts. I enjoyed becoming interested in a certain topic and having the time to dig deeper into the subject, without worrying that I would fall behind in another subject and fail a test.

This approach to learning is very similar to what I've encountered at Aquinas. I wasn't sure it would be so similar when I first came here. I didn't know how my experience being homeschooled would impact my academic and social life at Aquinas. I've found that my homeschool experience made me an independent thinker, which is essential at college. All the days I spent alone in my room, concentrating on studying and reading books, prepared me for the intensity of college classes. College also requires people to reach out to make friends, since we are not stuck in the same small building all day and don't share classes with the same people all the time. By being homeschooled, it was easier for me to be comfortable being on my own. I had to reach out to others to make friends. It's made college that much easier. I've also come in contact with a lot of fellow homeschoolers at Aquinas. We're not as uncommon as some may think.

Overall, homeschooling has benefited me at Aquinas. I haven't had any trouble with academics or making friends, which some critics of homeschooling may assume I would have. Whenever I do have the opportunity to mention I was homeschooled, many are surprised I was. In a way, I am not much different than any other college student. Everyone has their background; mine happens to be homeschooled.

# Having Faith at College

## Tyler Nadeau

Having faith is a challenge, especially for a college student. The stereotypical college student is one who goes out on the weekends, parties, and lives a foolish life where the most important aspect of life – faith - is forgotten. Ever since I have come to college it has been my responsibility to maintain my faith. Did I mention yet another struggle? I am not Catholic, and I attend a college where only Catholic masses are held for students to attend. I thought my faith was not "good enough" for a Catholic college, but I have fit right in and my faith has been welcomed and supported by Catholic friends, mentors and professors. Faith is a challenge, but one I will never give up on.

For the past three years, my studies have dominated every aspect of my life, unfortunately including my spiritual life. I was scared when I first moved to Aquinas. I thought I would be the only "non-Catholic" person and everyone would just look down on me. After orientation I immediately found out I was not alone, but I still had one thing on my mind: my roommate was a diehard Catholic.

It took a few months for him to accept we both make the same mistakes and we both serve the same God. Countless nights were spent discussing the topic of our faith, and I knew right then I had the best roommate in the world; someone who wanted to open up and share their faith story and allow me to do the same. The deepest conversation we ever had involved how God wants us to be honorable men. We talked about how the temptations of this world are so overwhelming that at times it is hard to remain faithful, so we created a challenge for each other, one where we were going to hold each other accountable for our actions.

This whole conversation started on the basis of confession in the Catholic Church and its necessity to be freed from sin. I argued my faith only says to ask God for forgiveness, whereas the Catholic's believe they must confess their sins to a priest before partaking in the Eucharist. What I did agree with is the fact we as humans should open up to one another and share our struggles with our friends. From that day on, my roommate and I had very high standards for one another. We expected to have daily conversations about the positive and negative aspects of our actions, thoughts, and words.

Once I got to know my roommate a little more, I decided to attend Mass here at Aquinas with him. It was nothing like what I had expected. I expected everyone to look at me as an outsider, someone whose faith wasn't as "good" as theirs. I knew I wouldn't be able to partake in the Eucharist and the thought of this made me feel alone and forbidden from having a connection to Catholics and God. I was wrong; everyone was so welcoming and appreciated my attendance. Right then I knew God had placed me at Aquinas not only to acquire one of the greatest friendships, but to see him through a different lens, one where he wanted me to trust him in all of my endeavors.

I also had one of the best experiences of my life on a spiritual retreat at Aquinas in November 2012. As I sat in a dark room filled with college students yearning to know more about our awesome God, I realized I was not the only person struggling with my faith at this point in my life. Every person in that room had a story to tell, and I knew right then that God wants to have a personal relationship with me and every other human being. I opened up to him, and my faith was renewed.

Challenges have come about since my faith renewal, but I am willing to fight the fight. I am willing to stay on the path less traveled. I want to read my Bible every day. I need faith in my life. The greatest thing about Aquinas is no one pressures you into any faith; you are accepted and loved no matter what denomination label you wear. My hope and prayer is God will continue to bless me and provide me with the opportunities of fulfilling and living my aspirations and faith, and ultimately to never give up on Him.

# Understanding Yourself

## Ashley Browe

Here at Aquinas, I really have begun to understand myself more. I have found my optimism and determination key aspects of my success. I have always had these traits, but it was not until I became a "Saint," that I truly began to understand my strengths. These strengths have helped me to the point I am at today and will only continue to give me the drive to reach my goals of becoming an Elementary Teacher and impacting the lives of children.

My optimism, or rather my belief that there is always something better around the corner, has helped me get from day to day. I know that even with a bad day, tomorrow is brand new and full of possibilities. It helped me as a child when I was diagnosed with Perthes Disease, a disorder in which blood circulation is cut off to the hip bone, causing deterioration of the bone. This caused multiple doctor appointments, crutches and even at one point, a wheelchair. I was an outcast, seen as different by my peers and even bullied. I remember not being able to participate in some of the field day activities and because of that, I was picked on. I had to sit to the side of all the activities, with a view of everything going on. At the time, it hurt watching everyone else having fun, but I made it my goal to be able to participate one day. I knew I would get to the point where I would have fun running and participating. Even with all the complications my Perthes Disease caused, I still kept my optimistic outlook, knowing that things can only get better from there. I pushed through the bullying, the surgeries and the numerous doctor appointments to now have minimal complications with my hip. Here in college, my optimism has gotten me through the toughest of classes; however I would not have passed without my determination.

Determination, by definition, is the firmness of purpose, or the drive to do something. I know I am very determined in what I do in life. My determination is what has gotten me through quite a bit of situations. It also happens to make me a bit stubborn at moments, as I have a difficult time giving up. Regardless, this drive to do things has gotten me to where I am today. Even with my Perthes Disease, I was determined to participate in basketball my senior year of high school. I remember coming home after practice in unbearable pain, but knowing that I could do it made it worth it. Maybe I was stubborn for putting up with the pain, but I was determined to complete the season. Overall, I would not have attended Aquinas College or played basketball in high school had it not been for my determination.

My two special attributes are a unique mix. They work together, giving me the need and want to continue with life. I know that many people have told me how infectious my optimism is, but they do not realize just how much that optimism influences my life. Also, without one of these attributes, I do not think I would be the same. They are so closely related, that the lack of my determination or optimism would feel like a part of me was lost. These two attributes drive me in my future and I know they will help.

Recently, my two strengths have gotten me through a lot. Every day, I am faced with a new challenge within life, but my optimism and determination to make it to the next day gets me through. Taking eighteen credits, working and observing in local schools can be exhausting and some days seem impossible, but I know that it will pay off later. One day, I was extremely busy with barely a minute to myself. I had a list, which seemed a mile long, but kept thinking, "I can do it. Today is only one day." I kept telling myself good things and the day actually turned out to be great, because I saw it in a positive manner.

Beyond the immediate future, I have the goal to impact children's lives. I plan to use my optimism to help a student who may be struggling see that they can learn and succeed. My determination will give me the drive and persistence to help the child, which is what some students need. They just need an adult to be on their side and go the extra mile for them. This is exactly what I plan to do and I will use my strengths to help students.

# Breaking Out of Your Shell

## Danielle Ames

My quaint little town of Caro, Michigan has been around for the majority of the last one hundred and fifty years. In the earlier period of its conception, my home was known for logging the large timber bearing trees within the area, and also for its sugar beet factory, Pioneer Sugar Co. While the logging industry subsided long ago, to this day you can still smell the unique odor that percolates out from the factory while driving down Main Street.

Ever since the beginning when I blessed my family with my birth, I have inhabited Caro. A large portion of my time since then has been spent sitting in a chair and earning a high school education. During this time, I met many friendly students at school and obtained one very close best friend, whom I met all the way back in my kindergarten class in 1997 and have remained in contact to this day. My best friend and I were complete introverts ever since the beginning of our relationship.

Only when we were in each other's presence would we ever speak out loud for more than five minutes. I always did well in school and answered questions when prompted, but other than succeeding academically, I lagged behind socially. For instance, a socially comfortable individual would have a cakewalk with an oral presentation in class. However, during my first oral presentation in high school, I could not have been more nervous. My whole body was convulsing with a tingle that ran up and down my spine. My eyes wandered around the room looking at anything inanimate that could not hold a stare. My thoughts were all tied up like a big ball of string and locked within the deepest part of my brain, unlikely to be found during my presentation and expounded upon to my fellow students. I quickly and messily made my way through that first presentation and my first experience speaking in front of my peers for a whole ten minutes. That's how I felt until quite recently, when I finally moved across the state and experienced an exciting and alarming new atmosphere in the magnificent city of Grand Rapids.

With my clothes and personal items all packed up, I moved here to study biology at Aquinas College almost two years ago. I was excited and eager as ever to learn more about biology and I was ready to take the next step towards a degree that would optimistically lead me to a promising career. However, my optimism halted for a brief period of time. While I felt I was ready to take on a new town with a new atmosphere, I was quite wrong. Caro was but a speck of dust compared to the size of Grand Rapids. The lively ambiance that encapsulated Grand Rapids ultimately startled me in the beginning. Being a farm girl, I was used to the quiet sounds of nature and the abundant greenery that I called home for my whole existence.

The people were quite different in Grand Rapids as well. Holding my metaphorical social shell in place as a defensive mechanism, as I did for the past eighteen years, I attempted to slowly let the new people and the environment into my life. I stumbled a lot in the beginning. Originally, my conversations would consist of a meager salutation along with some nervous small talk, just as they did in high school. In one instance, I started out eager to communicate with this openhearted girl who was sitting in the communal lunchroom. I greeted her with a spirited hello and then we prompted each other about our day. As the conversation started to develop further, I slowly returned back under my shell. My nervous tendency to think profusely about how another human being might perceive me; it has been a barrier blocking my social bloom for the last 18 years of my life. After my small conversation with this young lady, I sat in silence for the next fifteen minutes, which felt like forever, until I decided that I should probably go sit somewhere else to make less of a fool of myself.

Nonetheless, from that point on I have prevailed. Instead of being able to count my friends with one measly hand, I can now count more friends than will fit on both my hands and feet. After meeting others who let their spirits fly freely, spewing nonsense from their mouths and not caring what another person might say or think, I could tell they had found social peace. To follow, I finally let my thoughts spill out my brain and I could care less what others think about how I think and act. I am who I am and I can cheerfully say that I know these amazing people I have met will always be in my life from this point on. It would be crazy to let such incredible friends fall away. Starting out as a shy and reclusive individual I have now metamorphosed and cast my shell aside, just as a butterfly changes from a small, hidden caterpillar to a vibrant and friendly insect, to let my true colors shine.

# Fulfilling My Dreams

## Yasmeen Ahmed

Ever since I can remember I've had dreams about a career that I would love. When I thought about the future, that is what it revolved around. I always had a mindset that I had to make these dreams happen and then everything else could come after. As a child, I dreamt of being a dancer or a singer, but those lasted until age four, and then I found my real passion.

Even before I ever learned to read or write I would pick up books and flip through the pictures while making up my own story. I loved books, but what I loved even more was creating stories. When we started having literacy time in fourth grade I wrote so many stories, it was my favorite time of day. On Fridays we had the choice to read our stories out loud, and often I would get up in front of the class and read mine. Even at such a young age I prided myself on my writing. My stories and writing were what got me places; it was what people knew me for. I liked it that way.

There was a time when we were asked to do a research project on a possible future career. I wrote about being a journalist, I job shadowed and interviewed at the local news station, and to this day it is one of my fondest memories. I am still amazed that more than ten years later I haven't changed my mind about my dreams, with a few alterations of course, and I am still equally as passionate about fulfilling them.

Through the years I developed more dreams. I realized quickly my passion for traveling, and later in high school I started pursuing Spanish as a second language, as I have always desired to speak multiple languages. These dreams have led me to many places, and are continuing to make me the person that someday I hope to be.

To back up a little bit, my parents met after my dad moved here from Pakistan. Neither of my parents went to school, but my dad studied a little business and opened up his own store here in Grand Rapids. Both of my parents have always supported me in my dreams. My parents brought me up with a mindset that school would come before anything else, and my mom especially preached regularly that it was important to be an independent girl. It was drilled into my head that if I wanted to succeed, and I surely did, that I shouldn't let other little things distract me from that. My parents gave up more than I can ever imagine for me to be where I am today, someday I hope to give them something in return.

It's a weird feeling when your dreams start to come true. For almost twenty years I have held these dreams close to me, and I have been working towards them. When I started college, I continued to work hard and I have already fulfilled so much that I never imagined I would be able to. I started writing for *The Saint*, our student newspaper, which brought many connections my way. I developed much better writing, I met other people with similar aspirations, and I also started writing for a periodical outside of Aquinas to get more of my work published. I read my 'This I Believe' essay based on acceptance at a reading here at Aquinas. I also started some real traveling by taking a service learning trip to Maine, where I experienced new things and met so many great people. I realized even more, that making connections is what career and life building is all about. That experience was life changing and I truly could not have done it without the help of TRiO. While on the trip I was known for keeping daily journals of what we did in Maine and how we felt. At the end my notebook was passed around and everyone wrote down different 'Themes of Maine.'

Not much has changed, while many people lose sight of their true passions as they grow up, mine are only growing stronger. I still pride myself on writing, and I'm known for it by many people, I like it that way. Not only was I able to travel to Maine, but I recently was accepted into the Fall Study Abroad Spain Program. I'll be embarking on a new journey next September, and I also recently received a Study Abroad scholarship. After writing a persuasive essay for the scholarship entry on why I deserve the scholarship, I once again feel like my writing has taken me many places.

This summer I am applying for several writing internships, while I develop my communication skills working for the Aquinas Fund. I aspire to travel after graduating with an International Business and Spanish major, and journalism minor, while continuing to write, and hopefully someday even putting my fulfilled dreams and wisdom into a book, like I've always dreamed of.

I have struggled, it was hard at first not knowing how to get where I knew I wanted to be. Even today, I have second thoughts about what I'm doing because there is a lot of pressure on me, but there are two things that have always been present and those two factors have brought me through everything difficult. My passion and confidence in my dreams have made everything worth it, because I have chosen certain paths for those reasons, and now I am happier than ever, fulfilling my aspirations. Now I still can't believe the things that I have already done and fulfilled, and the dreams that are in sight at this point. They still feel unreal, and I never thought I'd have this many people behind me to help fulfill them, but I know I wouldn't be here without them. I can't explain exactly what it feels to fulfill my dreams but I know that it is the constant motivation to continue working hard and fulfilling more dreams.

# Being Normal

## Katelyn Padalino

I am a student at Aquinas College who is majoring in biology/pre-medical and minoring in music. When I was in my sophomore year of high school, I began having what is currently diagnosed simply as "chronic pain." This minor disability does interfere in my academics; however, I try not to allow it to define me too much. While I would say that I do have a disability, I attempt to make myself as "normal" as possible and adjust what I do to what is the easiest on me. While a lot of people my age are pulling all-nighters and having an erratic sleep schedule, I simply am not able to do that. However, by having a regular sleep schedule, I am able to be more productive during the day. I do not think I am making a huge adjustment; it is just easier on me to go to bed at a decent time, and to get up at the same time every day. I find that if I keep consistent on sleep/study schedules, and manage my time effectively, I am able to do more.

This also does not hinder the "service" and "community" aspects of life that the Dominican roots of Aquinas I hold so dearly. I volunteer at St. Thomas a few days a week, and am active in several extracurricular activities. My main extracurricular activity I do is technically a class, but it is a huge part of my life. I am a member of the Chamber Strings group.

While I do not feel like I have been hindered in my college experience, I cannot say the same about high school. My first year, I had excellent grades, and put as much into that as I could. Most of my sophomore year, I was doing very well, and had great grades as well. It was the second semester that was different. At the very end, I began having mysterious pain in my limbs, and they didn't really set on slowly. I literally was relaxing one day and it just began. It hit me fairly severely at first, and continually got worse. I went from doctor to doctor, and spent the first half of my junior year on homebound study, and the second half at home and half in an actual classroom. I was able to get through it (including two college level courses) pretty well. I also was on homebound study for part of the first semester of my senior year, and was part time the second half. I was able to overcome my obstacles by diligently working hard. There really is no substitute for working hard. I feel I proved myself to anybody that thought I just liked missing school, and eventually developed an "I don't care what you think about me" attitude about my whole situation. I am more than meets the eye.

I remember how helpful and supportive my high school principal was through the whole thing. He really went out of his way to make sure I graduated, and graduated to the best of my ability. Whenever we had an issue with me getting the runaround about being able to take my medication in school, or had an issue with a teacher not sending work down while on homebound, we were able to fall back on him, and he always took care of it. My homebound teacher was very good at politely going down to a teacher in person and telling them they had to send work down for me, if they were not. This was a huge part at how successful I was able to be in high school.

All in all, I don't consider myself different than everyone else. I see myself as having different needs to be the same. If there was one thing I would want to tell someone going through the same thing as me, it's keep going! No matter what, you can do whatever you want to do, just keep working at it, and you will be successful.

# To Serve

## Emily McAfee

When I first came to Aquinas I had no idea what our four charisms were. However, the more time I spent at Aquinas, the more I felt myself drawn to things related to service. A friend of mine decided to join Habitat for Humanity at Saint Stock, and I decided to do the same. Little did I know how big of an impact the club would have on my life.

Flash forward to April. I was almost done with my freshman year in college, and found myself wanting a position on Habitat's executive board for my second year. Although I had wanted to run for vice president, I was elected to be president! The fact that the upperclassmen had faith in me leading the club reassured me, so I accepted the role. As the summer quickly passed, I became more anxious for the upcoming year. I had no idea how to run a club! As nervous as I was, I had also been selected to be an Orientation Leader, and the confidence I gained from that helped the natural leader in me rise to the occasion.

I had a great experience being president. Running a club is unlike anything I had ever done. I had to get members, decide when to have meetings, organize fundraisers, and more. The responsibilities were more than I expected but it was worth it in the long run. I loved the feeling of helping out others, and I knew that I wanted more leadership roles in my life.

I will never forget one of my favorite builds. We were working on the day of the dedication of the home, and the family who would be moving in was there. Being able to talk to them and see how appreciative they were was an eye opening experience. The families who move into Habitat homes have a long process. They must first apply and show that they are in need. They also have to take classes on finance, home repair, and what it means to be a homeowner. Hearing the family's story that day only pushed me to go on more builds, and help more people. Habitat is so much more than giving someone a house; you are helping give someone their life back. I always thought I had this amazing connection with Habitat strictly because I loved giving back. However, an unfortunate event in my own life changed my perspective on many things and made me that much closer to Habitat.

During the spring of my sophomore year, I studied abroad. While I was out of the country, my family lost our home and had to move out. When they told me, my heart shattered into a million pieces. This was my childhood home, the only place I had ever known. I had so many fond memories from there. Every summer we would eat outside on our deck and have bonfires almost every night. Friday nights we had people over to play cards. I learned to cook in that house and I even had my first home renovation in that house. We re-did our kitchen one year, and my Dad let me take a sledge hammer to one of the walls we knocked down. Knowing I would never be able to step foot into it again was the worst feeling.

There are an estimated 100 million people in the world who define as homeless, and suddenly I was part of that statistic. Luckily, my family has great friends who they moved in with for a few months while they looked for a place to rent. By the time I got back to the States, we were already packing up to move into our new home. Most people aren't that lucky though. Families are forced to live on the streets or move in with relatives that don't have enough room. That's where Habitat comes in. That's why I am so passionate about working for the organization, and running the club on campus. I was re-elected to be president for my junior year, and I am planning on running again for my final year at Aquinas.

Coming into my first year of college, I knew I wanted to be involved but I didn't expect to be as involved as I am today. Although my schedule is sometimes hectic, I absolutely love how my college years have turned out. I don't get to sleep in anymore because of commitments, but lack of sleep and increased amounts of coffee are what define a college student, so I think I'm doing just fine.

# Finding Your Path

## Christian Baker

As a young child, my parents encouraged me with words that still ring in my ears: "Christian, you can be anything you want to be if you set your heart to it." Although it may seem cliché, the belief sticks with me to this day. So as a kid, Legos would transform into buildings and cars as I dreamt of being an architect. My hands zoomed from piece to piece creating a new masterpiece with each swipe. Then, my interest waned with the introduction of "Top Gun." Soon, the F14-tomcat with its retractable wing design and aerodynamics became the fantasy of my thoughts as I flew around the room. My dream of flying though came crashing down in the summer of 2006. A new dream, a much more plausible dream, grew from the ashes. On that humid day in August, my little brother received his diagnosis.

Rewind six years to the birth of Deegan, my little brother. His impeccable health and cute appearance rendered him irresistible to all. Jealousy pulsed through my veins as Deegan took the spotlight, the 'Only Child Syndrome' taking effect. Day in and day out, brotherhood soon became a part of life. Life fell into a rhythm like rain pattering on a windowsill. Then, the storm began to rage. This healthy young boy began to gradually go down-hill; first a stuffy nose, then a respiratory infection that wouldn't budge, then his stomach cramped in pain. The illness was undefined as various symptoms showed in countless body systems. His immune system battled long and hard, yet compared to his peers, his illness remained. The illness appeared three, four, five times more than the average child his age. Deegan's weight dropped, his skin was sucked tight around his bones like a vacuum sealed package. By the time my little brother was four he was very skinny and was basically skin and bone.

A diagnosis of Crohn's disease helped relieve the stomach pains and Deegan gained a couple pounds. This diagnosis maintained Deegan's health until his fifth birthday. As my parents' marriage fell into pieces, so did Deegan's health and he landed himself a warm bed in Helen DeVos Children's Hospital. His summer days belonged to the hospital floor while mine were spent in the sunny outdoors. Distractions filled my time to keep out the darkness that kept creeping in...my brother must survive...I could not lose my little brother. Three months later, a diagnosis appeared: Hyper IgM Syndrome. A bittersweet victory was obtained. Yes, a diagnosis, but one that needed much research. The words rang in my mind....Hyper IgM Syndrome...I feared that this diagnosis was not a means of treatment, but just a label to explain what my brother would surely die from. My parents explained that Hyper IgM Syndrome is a rare case of immunodeficiency. Deegan could live with the disease; he simply needed monthly immunoglobulin infusions in addition to antifungal medications. Relief washed through me, relaxing every nerve in my body instantly. Little did I know that I had gained an intense interest in the practice of medicine through my brother, Deegan.

My college courses have solidified my decision and made me more excited to pursue medical school. Microbiology taught me how certain pathogens infect individual host and how they spread. Genetics taught me how certain inherited diseases pass from one generation to another. The intellectually stimulating subject of Immunology, which is my favorite course, taught me how our immune system fights off so many different pathogens to keep people healthy. In my volunteer work at the hospital, patient interactions reminded me of the vulnerability of the hospitalized. Additionally, observation allowed me to see innovative procedures. My classes and volunteering at the hospital have helped me understand things in so many different ways to hopefully become a great doctor someday.

My little brother plays games with me now. He takes my Legos, building cars and jets, forming his own dreams. He imagines fighter pilots and life-saving missions. His monthly infusions continue, yet his smile reminds me of the life he is able to live. I thank the doctors that found out about his disease because, now that he gets his monthly infusions, he is one of the healthiest kids I have seen. Seeing him smiling and having fun with other kids makes me happy. My strong bond with my brother continues to be of the utmost importance in my life. He and I may get in fights all the time, but that is what siblings do. Every moment I share with Deegan creates a new memory that is held close to my heart. Although his illness is unfortunate, without Deegan, medicine may have been a dream I pushed aside. But now, I am thankful that my brother inspires me to chase my dreams. Interestingly, Deegan stands as my inspiration, yet he already sets the Legos aside and dreams big. Deegan looks up to me and sees his dream. He wants to be like me. He wants to become a doctor. He wants to be like his big brother. That is the humbling thing about my brother: he always reminds me that I can do anything I set my heart to.

# Living in Costa Rica

## Leah Nawrocki

I can remember applying to study abroad in Italy, Spain and Costa Rica. This was because I could not make a definite decision. I could not even decide if I would travel during the fall or spring semester, of my sophomore year. Yet, this was a decision I knew could be life changing.

With the help of a Spanish professor and the travel abroad director I was able to finally make a decision. They helped me realize that a spring trip would fit me better as a newer college student and Spanish major. This decision led me to spend the spring semester in Santa Ana, Costa Rica. And though I am paying my own way through college I received financial support to make this once in a lifetime trip a part of my life.

I spent my fall 2011 semester in the 301 level Spanish course in preparation for the 302 grammar course in Costa Rica. Other ways I prepared for this trip were to apply for a passport, attend group meetings and follow the very specific packing list I received. I was given my host family's name about a week before departing in January of 2012. I spoke to students who had previously traveled to Costa Rica, two of which had stayed with the same host family as me. Despite the excitement during the preceding week, departure brought me a new type of anxiety. This was because I was leaving everything I knew to speak a second language and live 2,276 miles from home.

Despite my nervousness I said goodbye to my dad at the first gate and gathered my second suitcase. I had already checked my first suitcase upon arrival. I walked apprehensively with one of the other Aquinas students. After going through the tedious security measures, all thirteen of us students and Professor Romero, made it onto both flights. Our arrival was no less chaotic than departure as we had to carry our four months' worth of belongings and navigate ourselves through the crowds. We were brought to our bus by Professor Romero and then quickly introduced to the program directors, Don Jorge Acevedo and his wife Dona Ana. I did not know it at the time but these two people would be very difficult to say goodbye to, four months later.

Our introductions to our host families were quick and after I had identified my new host parents Lady and Jorge, my suitcases were put into their vehicle. I was so anxious that I could not even answer my age in Spanish, a skill I learned in grade school. I had previously decided I had no preference of whether I would live with another Aquinas College student. This was a decision I momentarily regretted. Eventually I came to know my host parents extended family very well. They all became an important part of my life as I came to learn Spanish and appreciate Costa Rican culture.

My first couple of days in Costa Rica helped me get rid of all my doubts. Hikes in the mountains, a weekend stay at an all-inclusive resort and meeting new professors were all part of this once in a life time trip. I took full advantage of each opportunity, going river rafting, attending new art exhibits, taking countless photographs and spending time with my host family. I also stood under waterfalls, went banana boating and tried many new foods. I found that this opportunity was helping me better know myself.

A lot of things I learned and observed, reminded me of my life in Michigan. This was because the relationships my host family shared were a lot like those within my own family. I can specifically remember sitting at the Valentine's Day celebration with my host parents and their children. I watched them laughing at their two year old grandson who was pretending to play guitar. I also listened on many occasions to my host parents and their daughters reminisce about past family birthday parties and vacations. The pictures in their household were not the only evidence that they love each other very much.

My host family reminded me of life in Michigan in other ways too. They value family time, traveling and caring for others. Lady and Jorge made it a point to ask me about each group trip I took, about my friends, my homework and my personal opinions. This is no different than my own parents. They brought me more appreciation of the people in my life. Because of their generosity I felt very much at home in Costa Rica. My newfound gratefulness of different ways of life and the joy it brings has seriously changed me as a person.

Consequently, my life has never been the same since I made the commitment to live in Costa Rica for four months. This was not just a commitment but a new way of life in which I better grasped what is really important in life. Costa Ricans could not have summed up life better when they say that life is pure or great which is to say *pura vida!* This phrase is one I commonly use as I grow academically and spiritually. Speaking Spanish is now a permanent part of me as I can help others whose first language is Spanish. Having what I now consider family, in Costa Rica has led me to expand my relationships and my communication with the people who helped make my trip a once in a life time experience. PURA VIDA!

# Finding a Home

## Jessica McCormick

I walked slowly, my eyes wandering over the vast expanse of the campus that, as a freshman, I was learning to call my home. I absorbed the landscaping and structures around me, deep in a trance of conscious thought. I surveyed my new surroundings with great scrutiny. My attention to detail was important, because I knew that in a few short months, I would not have somewhere to be. Before too long, the campus that now seemed so warm and open and welcoming would be frozen, shielding itself from the cold by hiding under a thick quilted blanket of shimmering snow. I could envision the friends that I was already starting to make: home, safe and warm with their families, probably sitting in front of a fireplace or Christmas tree and sipping hot chocolate and eating warm sugar cookies.

As a homeless youth, school vacations were difficult for me. Usually, I was a social butterfly. But sometimes even weeks in advance, I would regress into a frightened caterpillar, curled up and clinging to any tight cocoon I could build around myself. I took on the more fragile characteristics of the butterfly, the wings on which hope and security rested upon easily smeared by even the lightest touch. All of my friends got excited about time off from school, sleeping in, and going home to see family. I sat back and watched as the stark reality of loneliness settled in. One by one, parents showed up, mothers eager to see and hold their children after a few months' separation and fathers carrying luggage in a way that I was sure seemed slightly aggrandizing. Between the panic and the loneliness, my delicate wings were left stiffly frozen.

Time passed, and my freshman year turned into my sophomore year. As I got more involved around Aquinas, I learned about some fantastic opportunities. During fall and spring breaks, I found opportunities to go on service learning trips with Campus Ministry. Christmas break was more difficult, but even when there were no solutions found, I learned to work with people around me to search for solutions for future students. Even though their lack of understanding could be upsetting, I learned to ease my own sharp attitudes and to be as patient with them as I asked them to be with me. I discovered that there is housing over the summer right on-campus, and it is in some ways easier than outside housing: all utilities are covered and there are no landlord-tenant altercations. Slowly but surely, I was starting to evolve from the fragile cocoon that enshrouded me.

Furthermore, as I got more involved, I found ways that I could use my experience to show others how they could get involved: how they could help, what they could change, and what some of the real issues facing homeless youth were. It is continuously amazing to me how unaware my fellow students are about the people in their own city, their own community, and in this case their own classrooms—people who are without families, without homes, and sometimes even without access to basic needs. However, what leaves me even more awestruck is the willingness to learn, to help, and to be involved that seems ingrained in my friends and classmates. Ultimately, they are the ones who helped me to find a future, emerge from my cocoon and take flight.

Eventually, my inner butterfly was released. Interestingly enough, it was not by finding the fireplaces where sugar cookies and memories were shared. Instead, I was freed by opening myself up to the people and opportunities around me. The secrets that had kept me bound within the confines of my cocoon turned into the sharing that could make a huge difference in my community. The beauty I found in sharing my experiences with others and opening my mind to experiences that they were willing to share with me was ultimately what helped me to spread my wings and fly.

# Being a Leader

## Thomas Serna

Leadership wasn't a strong attribute of mine when I went to White Cloud High School. I had never felt comfortable with expressing myself and sharing my own beliefs because I felt like no one would listen. However, a part of my self-confidence was also an issue. Believing in my decision-making and my own moral beliefs was difficult and I often kept these things to myself. So for most of my high school years, I kept quiet. It saddened me in a way, but I felt that I needed a catalyst to feel the confidence to pursue a leadership role that people would admire and believe. I didn't realize that going to Aquinas College would be the catalyst I was hoping for.

I was originally a part of AQ Psychology Club my freshman year, but I soon felt less inclined to stay in the club. I felt the need to leave AQ Psychology Club, but another club opportunity had risen up to my attention. A friend of mine had left Aquinas due to personal matters with the college. He was also the Game Club's President at the time. I thought if he was leaving the college, then what would become of the club? Was there anyone to keep the club going? I spoke to his girlfriend, who was the club's RSO Representative. She told me that other than herself, there was no one else on the club's Executive Board to run the club. The club had been suffering from an absence of members. More and more, the club was losing attention from the Aquinas College community.

I thought about the idea of having another club falling apart. I had little reason to be a part of a club that I didn't want to be a part of, but some inspiration sparked within me. I felt driven to take control of the club as its new President. I wasn't sure if I would completely express what I wanted the club to be as I saw fit, but I felt a need to try, not just for the club's survival, but to reveal the confidence that I wanted to shine from me.

I told the RSO Representative that I would temporarily take the role of President for Game Club. I had never been a leader of any club before then. After taking some time to invest in information on how clubs are run, including any resources that Game Club had, I decided to take the resources into my own hands and use what I had to make a difference for the club; to make a difference with what I believed in. I didn't think that my confidence would hold out for me, since I felt nervous about the idea, but I felt inspired to continue on.

I assessed the main weakness that the club faced: communication. Apparently, the club was losing contact with the members of the club, which explained the absence of its members. Communication wasn't my strong suit, but I decided to start with an e-mail that I composed for the members on the club's emailing list. To my surprise, I received a few replies. Some asked for new game ideas for the club. There were other replies for fulfilling the positions on the Executive Board, which needed to be filled. I couldn't believe that my email that I worked on for almost an hour to share my inspiration was being seen and taken seriously.

Eventually, I was able to establish meetings for the club. At first, the club had no visitors. Despite the absence of participants, I waited for each meeting in hopes people would arrive to the meetings. After a couple of meetings, people who had asked to be a part of the club's Executive Board decided to come, as well as normal members of the club. I shared my inspiration of ideas that I explained in the first couple of e-mails I had sent out. I was still nervous, but I felt even more inspired to keep sharing myself with the club and its members to keep the club afloat.

I was grateful with my confidence, as it had taken me quite a ways. However, I realized that I had little time on my hands and the club was soon becoming too much for me to handle. The presidency role was soon passed down to another member of the club and I left. Compared to my departure with AQ Psychology Club, I was able to express more of an effort to share my beliefs and ideals like I wanted this time around. The surge of opening up made me feel empowered to keep going and to keep making an impact like I believed that I could give. Even though I was only a part of the club for a short time and I felt somewhat saddened for leaving, I left with a bigger smile, knowing that I had succeeded in opening myself more and to my abilities.

# Managing Time

## Chelsea Maslar

My first semester at Aquinas College was full of uncertainty. I did not always know where to go for what I needed or how to get involved around campus. It took a while for me to adjust to a lifestyle away from home. Nonetheless, slowly during that year I began to feel a sense of belonging. Due to this familiarity, I started to manage my time in a way that enabled me to succeed academically. To my surprise, my schedule allowed me to still have time for myself. I spent this free time hanging out with new friends and getting off campus as much as possible because I did not have a car. Eventually, I started to realize I did not have any money to do anything. Due to this, I decided it was time to get a job.

I started looking for a job my freshman year at Aquinas College. I was limited to only looking on campus since I lacked a car. I applied everywhere. However, I was unable to find anything due to my lack of experience at the college. Finally my sophomore year, during which time I finally had my car, I obtained a job in retail at Justice in Woodland Mall. Justice is a clothing store for girls between the ages of 7-14. I did not know what I was getting myself into since I had no prior retail experience. What I have found from working there is that every girl likes to try everything on and act like they are in a fashion show, even if they walk out of the store without buying anything. This was fun to watch; however, it was never fun to put all the clothes back in a neat fashion just for the next customer to mess it up. Even with this frustration, I did enjoy working at Justice and the job allowed me to work around my academic schedule. On top of this flexibility, I only worked four to five hours during a shift. Due to this convenience, I was able to work on homework in the morning or at night during the days I worked. Obtaining this job at Justice also provided me the benefit of staying organized. In order to remember what days I had to work, I started to keep an updated calendar. Over a short period of time, I started to use this calendar for academic purposes as well. It allowed me to see when I was in class or at work and how much free time I had in between. It was hard at first to maintain this calendar since I had never used one on a routine basis, but I knew if I wanted to be successful academically, I could not wait to work on homework the night before it was due. Maintaining this updated calendar enabled me to visualize my schedule which allowed me to avoid completing tasks last minute and to always know when I was available. Due to this organization, I was able to create a schedule that allowed me enough free time to look for a second job.

During my junior year, I applied to be a peer mentor at Student Support Services. This job consisted of mentoring 10 to 15 freshmen among working in the office and planning and creating student events. Since I have an outgoing and friendly personality, I knew this job would fit me well. I did not obtain the position until second semester of that year. However, when I did receive it, I knew I could fit it in my schedule and apply the skills I learned from retail and academics to this new job. For instance, in retail it is important to ask open ended questions to get the customer talking about his or her needs. I used this skill when talking to my mentees. Most of them were shy and felt intimidated by an upperclassman. Therefore, to relieve this intimidation, I asked them open ended questions to encourage them to go beyond a yes or no response and talk about what they were having trouble with or what they needed help with. By doing this, among using other applied skills, I was able to add more value to my on campus job. As I started to become comfortable having two jobs, I realized I needed to reevaluate my schedule to fit in academics. Working both jobs throughout the week plus making time for homework was a challenge. I tried to stick to my calendar and accomplish what I needed to each day, but many of times after working all day with class, I did not feel like doing homework. However, what I came to learn was that if I procrastinated I would only do worse academically and I would be defeating the whole purpose of going to college. To resolve this lack of motivation, I started to write encouraging words on my calendar in order for me to keep in mind my overall goal of academic success. By doing this, I was able to keep in mind the purpose of what I had to do each day and why it was important to my overall success.

My third job I obtained during my senior year was a job I did not apply for. My advisor recommended me to an accounting teacher who was looking for an assistant. My advisor did so because of my academics and extracurricular activities, particularly my participation and success in the Aquinas College Idea Pitch Competition. This competition involves becoming an entrepreneur and pitching a short sales speech of a new product you came up with. During my sophomore year, I participated in this competition and was awarded second place. The competition is run by the accounting teacher who needed an assistant at the time. Since she already knew who I was, I did not even have an interview for the job. I was hired right on the spot. I loved working here because I had the opportunity to plan the Idea Pitch Competition after having been part of it. I'm glad I pursued this third job because it enabled me to become more familiar in the accounting field especially since I was a business administration major. It also looks great on my resume as an added experience. However, even with the benefits of this college part time job, I knew I could not work three jobs while still having time for homework throughout the week. Due to this, I knew I had to work less throughout the week. I decided since the mall is usually busier during the weekend, I would only work at Justice during that time. Since this decision, I was able to keep my prior homework schedule while working on the weekends as well. This decision to get a third job really tested my ability of time management. To this day, keeping a calendar is not one of my favorite activities but I feel it is necessary in order to maintain a balanced lifestyle.

Working three jobs while maintaining academic success did have its moments of stress. However, I have learned to organize my weeks and stick to what is planned for each day to achieve success. I believe the most important skill I learned was time management. Without it, I would not have been able to maintain such a busy lifestyle. With time management, I have also learned to stay organized. With this organization, I set realistic goals each day to achieve long term realistic goals. I believe it is important to know when too much is too much, but to also always push ourselves to greatness and to never stop striving for success even if we have reached our long term goals.

# Interning in Chicago

## Sarah Robinson

Chicago is great. It's full of awesome art, great restaurants and busy people who always seem to be on the go. If you're not from Chicago or have never even visited, it could feel like a different country. I mean there are places like Chinatown, Little Italy, Greektown and many more.

For one of my classes we went on a neighborhood visit. Basically our class is assigned a certain neighborhood within Chicago and we visit it as a class a few times. Our neighborhood visit was to a Puerto Rican area. The first visit we toured the area. Another visit our class volunteered by unloading and sorting a truckload of food to give to the poor. During the tour, our guide pointed out some of the locally owned restaurants. Afterwards, I was hungry and was interested in trying one of the restaurants he pointed out. Truthfully I wanted to go in and eat as soon as he pointed them out earlier but I held out. A classmate and I ended up grabbing a bite to eat at a locally owned restaurant called Nellie's. They are known for their coconut oatmeal, which I tried and was not disappointed. The menu is a blend of American and Puerto Rican foods. It was a great find and I liked it so much I went back the next day to have the breakfast buffet where I indulged in all the other great breakfast items like french toast, fried plantains (friend bananas), hash browns and of course I enjoyed the coconut oatmeal once again. If I hadn't been in Chicago as an intern who had an, "I'm eager to see and experience everything," mindset about the city, I probably would not have entered the mom & pop restaurant. But because I experienced the Puerto Rican neighborhood with my class, I felt as if there were somewhat of a safety net around anything I decided to explore on my own outside of the tour. I'm so glad I did decide to eat at Nellie's because I was able to enjoy really great food and support a local business at the same time.

I have to say, one thing I'm getting my money's worth is, my U-Pass, which gives me unlimited access to Chicago's trains and buses. As a part of the Chicago Semester program I received my CTA U-Pass within my first week of orientation. Learning how to navigate the city is no easy task for someone like me, who's never had to use public transportation on a regular basis. It's not a foreign concept to me however, because I've been abroad and had to trek around via public transportation, but relying on trains to commute to my internship every day was something new for me. For some people it comes naturally and for others, like me, it's something you have to work at to get a good handle on it. Try having to ride two different trains to work every day. You better pay attention at the changeover because you might just hop on the wrong train. Yep, that happened to me.

I was extremely tired and disoriented one particular morning and so mindlessly used to my routine that I accidentally got on the first train that came by me. But as I was sitting on the train, I realized it hadn't stop in a while. Then I it dawned on me, I got on the wrong train. Great! I quickly glanced up at the train stops posted above the door. I was on the purple line and I needed to be on the brown line. I had to get off, catch the train running in the opposite direction, then wait for the brown line train to come in. Luckily I left extra early that morning and was not late but man did I feel dumb.

Interning in Chicago takes getting used to and keeps you on your toes. Having studied abroad in Ireland prior to living in Chicago, I already gained a sense of independence that gave me the ability to bounce back from taking the wrong train. After living thousands of miles away from home for four months, it's not surprising I learned how to live and function on my own and became more independent. What the two experiences have in common is my main drive to explore and experience new things in new places. I'm strangely comforted by foreign experiences, both overseas and within the States. Living in Tully Cross, Ireland is quite different than living in Chicago, Illinois. In fact they are complete opposites. But because I studied abroad, I feel it was easier for me to endure living and interning in Chicago. Aquinas has given me the opportunity to experience all of this. I've been able to learn and grow in ways that are both frightening and exciting and I will cherish them for years to come.

# The Optimist

## Cecilia Kellogg

When I was in fourth grade, we all learned many different things but there was one thing I discovered that stuck with me until this day. One early spring morning, we started to learn the difference between seeing the world in a positive view or in a negative view. We were learning about being optimistic and pessimistic, and how they affected everyday life. The teacher gave us the "glass half empty / full" speech and that odd suspicion of the way your writing tilts up or down, to determine which side we were closer to. Through all these suspicions, I learned what it feels like to be an optimist in life.

From that day I strived to become an optimist at the age of nine, to make my glass always half full, knowing that seeing life at that point of view was beautiful. Now, ten years later, the road to becoming an optimist was long, hard and still not quite finished but someday will be. The reasons why I strive to be an optimist now are different than they were when I was a bright eyed fourth grader when I couldn't picture being anything else but positive about life choices and the things brought forth every day.

At nine years old the idea of optimism brings different actions than at twenty years old. The stepping stones for me at the beginning of my journey had struggles and accomplishments on a small level, for example learning that a best friend moving schools can still be contacted and new friends can be made. It was also shown that spelling bees can be won through practice even when they are lost the first time around. This point in my learning was seeing the positive in small things that most adults have already learned.

As I grew older I started to have to dig at points in time to find positive points in life. For as everyone has come to learn, with older age come bigger problems and responsibilities. My biggest test of being an optimist and having a positive outlook on life would be 9th and 10th grade of high school, some of the hardest times of a person's life. Having the struggles of finding yourself in many different aspects whether it is school, work or home life brings pessimism to many students. Along with these problems the biggest struggle of "looking for the bright side" in my life so far came when my family broke apart from everything I had known and grown up with. Fighting through that for a year was the largest test of my optimism, wanting to give up on everything, but with still pushing myself with optimism is the only thing that got me through.

Starting my freshman year here at Aquinas College was another real test of optimism and to determine if it could be sustained through the hardest points in life. The first couple weeks are the most difficult for freshman. I could relate and I truly believe the only way I made it through was the decade of being optimistic and how greatly it contributed to my life.

Adjusting from high school to college life was where I was tested the most. Being a first generation college student with no support from my parents to pay for debts to school brought a hardship on me. The fact of working 20 plus hours and having 18 credits of school just dragged me into the ground, feeling like I could never catch up no matter how hard I tried. Trying to fight through this while adjusting to the new study habits and making new friends was one of the hardest struggles I've been faced with. Every day I made sure to take ten minutes before I fell asleep to think about how eventually with pushing through this that it would be worth it and end up right in the end. This mindset was the only thing that got me through that year and into the next, where the work hours are less and the classes I'm passionate about are more abundant.

This attribute of optimism is applied to my everyday life here at Aquinas, as a TRiO member, a friend, a student and an individual. I believe that this attribute has and will continue to prepare me for my future goals by accepting the steps I need to take to get there and not giving up if they are not easily accomplished or clear from the start. I believe that this contributes to success and well-being; you need to have an optimistic view on your life and the future that soon will behold it.

When thinking back to being nine years old and that day I learned about these attributes, I would have never imaged that this simple lesson would bring me so far in life and change the way I would view and accept. The choice to be optimistic about daily life, the small and big choices that come along with it, has brought me so far in life I couldn't picture ever going back. The life of an optimistic person is a bright one.

# The Ability to Adapt

## Mayra Monroy

Not everyone has the chance to do something great. To travel, to meet new people, to experience this whole new life. I was thrust into that form of experience at age 9. Up until then, I grew up in the same house my parents did, going to the same school, living on the same block as my best friends in a growing central Texas town. I had grown accustomed to this life. When my father was moved to a new facility for his job, it hadn't occurred to me the cost of this. On a warm Tuesday morning in April, my parents approached me to discuss this new opportunity. As expected, I was against it. This was my life, my home; everything about me was tied to this house, this neighborhood, this city. The thought of moving somewhere I had never heard of, in a completely different part of the country, was the worst thing I could think of. Despite this, my parents convinced me to try something new. As terrible as it sounded, I figured I had no choice. The next day, our house was packed in cardboard boxes, our cars loaded up with them, a moving truck en route to a new home located in some place I had never even heard of; Grand Haven, Michigan. So I left my old life, at age 9, to travel cross country to this new location, to new possibilities.

My first day at this new elementary school wasn't the easiest, being that I was brand new, knowing no one. It was difficult at first, but I eventually adapted, and then I began to fit in, making new friends, new memories. On the first day, I met my best friend. She asked if she could borrow a pencil. Anxious and slightly awkward, I lent her one, hoping that maybe she would be my first friend at this new school. This was the start of a friendship that would last for years to come and still does today. I didn't know it then, but in that class I met my life-long best friend, my college boyfriend, and a teacher that would be my favorite for years to come.

My adaptability played a big role in this drastic change. Not everyone can adapt so quickly or so well. However, I was given no choice. I had to work with what I had. We stayed in that town for 2 years, before moving once again to a new city, to be closer to my father's job. Again, I started over, in a new school, with people I've never met. This would happen again, 3 years later. Every time, I was able to adapt and this was my strength. My ability to adapt let me fit in more; it gave me the ability to make friends faster.

This ability to adapt is an attribute that I believe is important to seek in people. The world and environment are always changing, so nothing really stays the same. As humans, we seek to avoid change, to dislike it. However, when things do change, you have to be able to adapt. My ability to adapt so quickly was something I had to learn. Due to this, I benefited from it. I've had to adapt in living situations all my life, so moving into a dorm with someone else, sharing some aspects of my life, wasn't something I had difficulties with. Sure, we fight, we argue, we eat each other's food on accident, but any conflict that I have with my roommate is resolved. Before Aquinas, I never shared a room with someone. I was an only child for 13 years of my life, so the idea of having to share personal space with someone else wasn't appealing. I decided to enter the school year with an open mind. Luckily, I've adapted to the living situation I was thrust into.

At Aquinas, I plan on majoring in Communications while minoring in Journalism. Communication is the study of how humans communicate, how they interact with themselves and with others. The human mind is always changing, so my ability to adapt is important in understanding that behaviors and methods of communication are always changing, but if I can develop an understanding of it, I can develop my own conclusions. I've always been fascinated with how people communicate and how their behaviors influence others. Adaptability is observing the behaviors of others and their communication, and adapting to that. My attribute will suit me well in pursuit of my major, as it will develop a deeper understanding of human communication. I hope to pursue a career in something journalism related, as I love writing and news. The world is always changing and everyone should be informed. Having a global perspective is what I hope to gain before my time is up.

Not everyone can get the opportunity to travel, meet new people, and experience new things. I know several people who have never left the state. I got to experience this at a very young age. I learned that not everything stays the same, but I have to be ready to take it on. Adaptability has given my life a swirl of endless possibilities.

# Getting to Ireland

## Shelby Wittum

My rain-pants *swished* as I adjusted my legs on the wide boulder I had been sitting on for the last half an hour. I picked at the slippery moss that was a vibrant green. I was about 15 yards from the shore thanks to low tide. The wind blew and it was over cast skies, but I smiled as I pulled the hood of my raincoat back up over my knit hat. A few friends were wandering back on the pebble shore. The windy North Atlantic engulfed any noise they were making. My solitude gave me time for a brief reality check; I had made it, it was real. I had been dreaming of a semester in Ireland since I was a senior in high school; I wanted to travel and experience life outside my West Michigan bubble. I longed to meet new people, taste new foods, and learn how to live life differently. Now three years later I was actually getting into the Irish groove of life. It was late February and I could still feel the rush of emotions I had during exam week in December.

Exams didn't feel so intimidating when I knew what adventures awaited me after Christmas. It was a difficult limbo between staying motivated to do well that week, and just throw my hands up in surrender. To increase my anxiety, I was anticipating the results of The Gilman Scholarship that week. I would be getting on that plane on January 9th whether I got the money or not; nothing would stop me from leaving once I was accepted into the program. I wasn't always this confident in my decision to go. The repercussions of my bank account kept me questioning my dream. My mom however, never once raised a question, but kept encouraging me that any extra loans acquired would be worth it. The $4,000 would allow me to relax a bit more while in Europe, maybe even indulge a little, and not come home to a totally empty bank account. It wasn't the only scholarship I had applied for. I searched high and low for any money dedicated to students studying abroad. I made videos, begged for reference letters, sent in essays, and would have jumped through hoops of fire if that meant an organization would help me fund my study abroad.

The call from the International Programs director at Aquinas finally came midway through finals week. She didn't make any small talk. She was too excited and jumped right to the point. I had won the Gilman Scholarship and would be receiving a check of four grand by the end of December. That check could go right to my student account at Aquinas and I would be reimbursed for what I had already paid. I almost dropped the phone, my eyes blurred with tears and I no longer cared where I was or who was looking. Relief and joy spread through my entire being and I started making feeble attempts at thanking Joelle for everything. Instead of actually expressing gratitude I think I just squealed and whimpered.

On the plane taking the 20 of us from Newark, New Jersey to Shannon, Ireland the squealing and whimpering in excitement became quick breaths of panic. I never questioned what I was doing or why, but I started to worry about everything I was leaving behind. How much would change while I was gone? Would my mom be okay for that long without me? What if my grandpa died and I couldn't come home for his funeral, could I ever get over that? The screen in the headrest in front of me displayed the plane's flight progress. The miles between Newark and me increased slowly as did my worrying. The entire six-hour flight was wrought with twinges of excitement and nervousness.

The plane touched down and there was rain outside my window. But it wasn't a bad omen; it was a rain full of life and new culture in every drop. We were welcomed through customs with hearty, thick accents that made my ears strain and my heart beat faster. The first Irish woman I talked to made me realize that I had finally arrived! I was free of my long awaited dream and only adventures and discovering lay before me. My worries were filed away and excitement took over. This new chapter in my life was here at last and I was so ready to live it to the fullest.

# Moving On

## Jill Straub

*"Character cannot be developed in ease and quiet. Only through experience of trial and suffering can the soul be strengthened, ambition inspired, and success achieved."* ~ Helen Keller

Underneath the bright lights and in the cold, sterile air, the young, fresh-faced nurse quickly shows the mother, writhing in pain, her newborn baby. The nurse doesn't gently hand the baby over to the mother as she should; instead, she allows the mother to take a quick glimpse at her new child and tells the mother in a panicky tone, "Here's your baby. It's a girl." And, then the nurse whisks the baby away, not even allowing the mother the soft touch of her baby's skin. The baby is rushed to the incubator, which is awaiting the newest arrival that cries to be nursed back to health. As the baby girl lies in the protective cover of the incubator, hooked up to a web of slender tubes crisscrossing each other to monitor the heart rate and provide oxygen, the mother cries for days. She cries so hard that she is moved to a private room where her tears won't prick the bubble of joy the other new mothers feel as they gaze into their baby's sleeping faces.

The baby girl survives, and the mother stops crying. At least, not as hard and for not as long. Now, it is time for the baby girl to cry, but every time she does her mouth opens, her eyes scrunch up. But no sound comes out. Her vocal cords are paralyzed, and she cries like this for the next three months. After several months pass, the swelling of her spine relaxes and slowly begins to fade. Sound begins to finally escape her mouth, and her clenched fists start to relax and uncurl themselves. But, her tiny legs never do kick again as they did the brief moment before her spinal cord was so savagely torn. The extent of the damage could now at least be determined, and it was permanent. The baby girl, the mother, the father, and the older sister would all have to learn to pick up the shattered pieces of tragedy and move on.

I would have to learn to move on, and to somehow create a life for myself that wasn't always--and still isn't always--welcoming to differences. The less than perfect. The outcasts. The invalids.

It is an able-bodied world. There is no doubt about it. Just ask anyone with a significant physical disability, and you'll get an earful. And, it's unfair. It's unfair that I sit in a wheelchair, while the person next to me gets to walk without even thinking about it. It's unfair to my father who wakes in the middle of the night, thinking he can hear me walking down the hallway. Only to find out that, once again, it is a delusion. It's unfair to my mother who has spent so many years caring for me, sacrificing for me, hurting for me. It's unfair to my sisters who may have felt guilty over having something they knew I never could. But, most of all, it is unfair me. I could spend my life complaining that it's not fair, but I choose not to. I choose to move on.

I received my first wheelchair when I was five. Before that, I crawled everywhere, hanging onto my mom's ankle. As she walked, I dragged along. Of course, I only did that at home. In public, my dad carried me everywhere, or I sat in a stroller--a special one for children who couldn't walk. But, once I received my first wheelchair, I could start living a more "normal" life. And, my parents began taking my sisters and me on trips...Los Angeles, Florida, Mexico, Canada,

Washington D.C., Virginia, Arizona, Gettysburg, and Spain. The one constant in every adventure was art and history. They exposed us to rich culture and essentially, to learning. I became a pretty voracious reader, and books were not discriminative against me. I may not have the fortunate blessing to walk, but books don't care. Through my books and through my travels, I learned. I absorbed knowledge that will sustain my mind and my spirit for a lifetime.

My thirst to learn whets my appetite to move on. It became my touchstone in life, and it redirected my focus off my struggles. It gave me a way to cope. Education brought me success and hope, as I finally finish thirty years of schooling, give or take a few years.

But, in the end, my challenges also gave me something else: patience and perseverance. In a culture of tragic instant gratification, I understand that true success is earned through patience and persevering. Perhaps, possessing those attributes make up, in a small way, for what was lost.

# A Major Exodus

## Julie Bevins

It is my freshman year in college, and I am running late for my 9am chemistry class. I live in the dorms in the valley, which means I have to walk down a steep hill and then up a doggone mountain to get to the main part of campus. For some reason, I recall the passage from Scripture where Moses goes up to receive the Ten Commandments, and I think: *I am going to miss my meeting with the Law.* I glance at my watch, and my backpack grows heavier with the realization that I am now definitely going to be late and will be forced to slink past my professor as he pauses significantly in the middle of his lecture to watch me huddle into a seat in the back row. I am weighed down by this impending embarrassment, lodged beside the three thousand ton chemistry textbook (which I practically had to sell my kidney to purchase) and the burden of my academic scholarship pressing against my spine. I am failing this course, I am sure of it, and if I do, what will that mean? Will I lose my scholarship? What will my parents think? And all my relatives and my teachers and my friends and all those people who seem to think I was smart enough to deserve this money when now it is becoming evident that I am a giant fraud? What am I doing here anyway? I am carrying this load with me up the mountain and into the classroom, where I attempt to surreptitiously pull it off my shoulders and plop it onto the floor beside my desk. I am neither unobtrusive nor quiet enough to feel as if my effort to Ninjaslide into class has been effective, and I quickly prop my gargantuan textbook in front of my face to hide. The instructor drones on in an unintelligible language, while my neighbors push their pencils about on notebooks as if transcribing something fantastic. At least, that's what it appears everyone else is doing. In self-defense, I start to write angst-filled poetry around the chapter headings in my chem book. In a flash, it comes to me: *You are not pre-med. You are an English major. It does not matter if everyone else thinks you will never find a job. You are not going to keep taking classes like this. If you do, you will die a slow and terrible death.* Because I have received this incredible bolt of lightning, I look around to see if anyone else has felt the impact. It appears nobody else has been moved by my epiphany. The professor continues to speak in a foreign tongue and the pencils move in their scratchy dance, while two seats over I notice a guy in a red baseball cap has fallen asleep and is drooling on his desk. I glance at the clock. The professor, who has something very important to finish saying, has already gone two minutes past the class end time, and the natives begin shuffling restlessly. In the row behind me, I hear someone whisperingly intone, *Let my people go,* and the students around me muffle their laughter. At last, our instructor waves a dismissal, and we uncurl ourselves from desks to roll toward the door. But my heart is already halfway down the mountain and back up the hill, singing the old hymn I have stolen from enslaved people who keep hope alive: *Free at last, free at last! Thank God Almighty, I am free at last!*

# Asking for Help

## Brian Parsons

2.3. Two. Point. Three.

My entire first semester of college had been neatly defined by two numbers and a punctuation mark. And what those numbers told me was that I failed. Maybe not according to the University standards, but in my mind those were the scarlet numbers that defined who I was. A fraud. A scam artist. And while classmates around me shared their successes I sat numbly wondering how I was going to tell my parents, namely my mom, what went wrong.

How do I tell my mom, the lady who dropped out of high school when she was 16 to raise my sister on her own and worked three jobs before having me at 23 about these grades? The same lady who went back to school to earn her GED in her late 20s, and continued on until she did everything but defend her dissertation for a PhD at just under 50. How do I explain to her that school suddenly became hard? That the sacrifices she and my step-father endured to afford to send me to an expensive liberal arts school was met with a 2.3?

I told myself this wasn't supposed to be happening to me. Growing up I was defined by school success. That became my identity. I was placed in the Gifted & Talented class as a first grader. My mom had me doing vocabulary workbooks in elementary school, which I realize sounds like the nerdiest thing ever, but I liked them. I love taking tests. Give me a Meyers-Briggs, an ACT test, IQ test, a Strengths Quest inventory, or whatever and I want in. Why? I have no idea. Probably because of my love of competition but probably because I had success at it.

That's who I was. But that 2.3 meant I had to redefine myself. Suddenly I had to deal internally with the notion that I wasn't as good as I thought I was. For an 18-year-old struggling with identity issues and trying to figure out the course I wanted to take after college, I suddenly had to deal with this slap in the face.

The worst part was I had even tried to create a schedule intent on being successful. I tested into French 2 after four years of high school French and the first week we jumped right into passé compose and I knew I was in trouble. The University required Calculus for the math component and since I just took Calculus as a senior I enrolled in that class and realized everything I learned the previous year was covered in the first eight weeks in college. Gulp. So if I couldn't hack classes that I had a solid background in, what was I going to do when I started taking classes that were completely foreign to me?

But the hardest part of that first semester? I didn't know why I had struggled. How do I fix a problem with no obvious solution? I was studying. I was keeping up with the readings. I was highlighting everything. I was taking notes in class. In short, I was doing everything I thought I needed to in order to be successful. But over Christmas break, in that moment of realization of what my efforts had earned, I cried. Uncontrollable sobs. Quietly. Alone.

Eventually over that break I faced my parents and told them my grades. They were upset, but didn't yell. They definitely reiterated what the tuition costs were and if I didn't improve we might be debating other options for the next year. One result of our discussion was being placed on a parent-imposed 'probation' which meant I was forced to seek guidance to improve my performance the following semester.

What I had to learn, and accept, was that I wasn't prepared. I needed help. I needed to give up this hero complex that said I had to suffer and triumph all on my own. That was a hard step. I tend to be a more introverted person when it comes to projects. I have control issues. I know this. But once I could get over myself for a second and accept guidance from friends who showed me their study habits, how they took more effective notes, and to learn from the academic resource center on campus, I actually felt my confidence improving.

In the Disney movie of my story I would tell you I made Dean's List that next semester with the coaching I received. Alas, no. But I improved to a 2.8 and my parents let me stay at DePauw. The semester after that I eclipsed the 3.0 barrier, and for the next five semesters of my college career, I hovered around that mark. I could accept that. That's what my energy and efforts had earned. Was I anywhere near being valedictorian? Not even close, but I was proud of myself because that was my best. Most importantly, I was unburdened from trying to define my self-worth through numbers, percentiles, and class rankings.

Isolating myself caused me to struggle. Only once I learned to seek help from others did I find my success.

# Without a Map

## Ann Karasinski

Wearing the new maize and blue sweatshirt I'd recently purchased from the bookstore, I arrived ten minutes early for my first college lecture. I found an aisle seat near the back of the large auditorium in the old central campus building I'd scoped out the previous day. I tried to swallow the giant knot in my stomach, but still, I felt like I was going to puke. I'd been a good student in high school, a regular on the Honor Roll, but I felt out of place here. At eighteen, I didn't know who I was or even who I wanted to be. I had simply applied and was accepted to the only university that my dad wanted me to attend.

The auditorium slowly filled to capacity, but I maintained a narrow focus, scared to look around and reveal myself as a foreigner, someone who didn't belong with "real" college students. Somehow, I knew that the safety of my high school identity—a quiet, compliant worker— didn't translate to this strange new culture. My dad had attended the *other* state school as a beneficiary of the GI bill, surprising himself and his family with his academic prowess, and making him a first generation college student. But now, I was second generation, with the added pressure of fulfilling my dad's dreams of even greater success. Unfortunately, I didn't have a map to this foreign land, and I didn't speak the language.

The professor entered from a side door and stood in the well of the room, distant and stiff. He was old, wearing something dark, and he had glasses and white hair and a beard. He instructed us to look to our left, and then to our right. His voice was flat and dry, a barren desert, where I wandered alone and afraid. "One of these people," he said, "will not make it. One of these people will fail." I thought that everyone knew he meant me, that *I* would be the one to fail, to disappoint my parents.

If I had been older or more savvy, I might have considered that many of the other freshmen were scared too. But I was young and not savvy about anything. My mother was a hundred miles away, and my new home was a shared cinderblock space in a north campus dormitory, accessible only by a regular shuttle bus. There were other students from my high school attending the same university, but they lived in the more popular dorms on the hill, and we hadn't been friends anyway. In the few days since my arrival, I'd met my roommate and the friendly girl from across the hall; otherwise, I didn't know anyone. I preferred to explore the world through stories and books, and I comforted myself with Earnest Hemingway and soft-serve ice cream that flowed endlessly in the cafeteria.

The freshman courses I took didn't inspire me, and I continued to wander, an academic nomad, unsure of what I should study. If things came easily—languages and social sciences—I discarded them, thinking them unworthy, and instead, I punished myself with difficult subjects— organic chemistry, calculus, physics—challenges that I thought were expected of me, and things that reinforced my insecurity. My professors and graduate teaching assistants assigned grades to my loneliness and misery, and when the first report card arrived at my parents' home, addressed to me; I hid it under a pile of socks in a dresser in my childhood bedroom. Privately, I begged my mother to let me leave the university, to transfer to a different college, something smaller and closer to home. She listened, but I knew the expectations hadn't changed, and I limped through the rest of the year.

During my sophomore year, with a year of freshman growing-pains under my belt, and a small measure of increased confidence and maturity, something interesting happened: I learned how to learn. I discovered the difference between rote memorization and higher-level thinking, and I began to master requirements and choose courses more wisely. I decided on psychology as a major, refined my interests within its discipline, and developed plans for graduate school. I had not only learned the language of college, I found my own voice.

Many years later, I took several classes at Aquinas College to maintain my certification as a school psychologist. I was one of only a few adult students in a class of undergraduates, and I was reminded of my freshman year and how far I'd come in my academic journey. Even though I was a stranger in the class, I was no longer afraid, and I reveled in the freedom I had to learn and to explore information and share knowledge.

In Meredith Hall's memoir, <u>Without a Map</u>, she shared her own first-day-in-college experience. She was a non-traditional student, but she was a freshman too. A full-grown adult and single mother of young sons, Hall described the same fear I'd had at eighteen, the fear of failure, of not belonging, and it made me wonder if there really is a "traditional" student. After all, aren't we all the same in our needs and desires, and yet unique in our skills and life experiences? When we are born, we instinctively know how to cry, but it takes time and experience to find our voice.

# Acknowledgments

First and foremost, we would like to thank all of the TRiO students in our program who shared their stories and themselves with the world. This authenticity is not easily achieved and for them to be their raw, emotional selves deserves an extreme amount of gratitude. In addition, a big thank you to Devon Klomp, who was responsible for the cover design of this book.

We also need to thank Gary Karasinski, June Stevenson, La Tonia Plunkett, and Jill Straub who helped us in generating excitement amongst our students to be engaged in a process like this. We are truly blessed to work in an environment where our supervisor and fellow colleagues encourage us to try new ideas and innovative ways of supporting our students and building our community.

To the Aquinas Community at large for providing the content for a lot of what our students shared. Aquinas College is a special place where students truly feel connected and create a home for themselves while they are here. In the narratives that were shared in this book, it's obvious the love our students have for this institution and the learning opportunities it provides them.

Brian Parsons, Ann Karasinski
& Julie Bevins